The Advisory Services Edge

Your Road Map to Transform and Grow Your Accounting Firm

L. Gary Boomer CPA.CITP

The Advisory Services Edge
140321-001

Published by:
90-Minute Books
Newinformation Inc
302 Martinique Drive
Winter Haven, FL 33884
www.90minutebooks.com

Published in the United States of America

ISBN-13: 978-1507785928
ISBN-10: 1507785925

For more information on 90-Minute Books including finding out how you can
publish your own lead generating book, visit www.90minutebook.com or call
(863) 318-0464.

Here's What's Inside…

Introduction

The Advisory Services Edge!

Jack Dixon said, "If you focus on results, you will never change. If you focus on change, you will get results."

Due to technological advances and commoditization of traditional compliance services, the accounting profession is on the cusp of great change. Firms who want to stay relevant and ahead of their competition are looking at moving their organizations from one of billing by the hour for compliance services to the more lucrative and higher valued advisory services.

I have been sharing the strategies on how to transition with my clients. Here are a few of the key components we cover in the book along with selected examples in the appendix.

- The Plan

- The People

- The Unique Processes

- The Pricing Matrix

- The Technology Platform

This book is the result of the learning and experience of helping dozens of our clients make the shift successfully from compliance to higher value advisory services. It is a quick read and one that will contribute to your success and make you future ready. Think 10 X. It is more exciting and quickly addresses the changes you should make in your firm. It will help you attract and retain better employees and clients.

What follows is a transcript where I walk you through the challenges and the strategies you face when making this transformation.

Enjoy the Book!

I hope this book educates you and helps change your way of thinking about offering advisory services and encourages you to take the leap to focusing on better and more rewarding opportunities. What have you got to lose?

To Your Success!

Gary Boomer

The Advisory Services Edge!

Susan: Good afternoon, this is Susan Austin and with me today is Gary Boomer, CEO of Boomer Consulting, Inc. Welcome Gary.

Gary: Hi, Susan. Glad to be here.

Susan: We are going to talk about your book *The Advisory Services Edge: Your Road Map to Transform and Grow Your Accounting Firm.* Why did you want to write this book?

The Changing Environment

Gary: I have been in the CPA profession for a long time, been a partner in an accounting firm and I have seen the direct impact technology has had on our profession. I want CPA firms to be able to leverage this technology, to help make them future ready. I think right now is one of those transformation periods where CPAs and their firms really have some distinct opportunities ahead.

They are also faced with many challenges and one of those challenges is how to grow and how to maintain relevance in their service area. I really wanted to explain what is becoming clear to me as we go forward of where those opportunities are, and how firms are going to have to change in order to take advantage of those opportunities.

I think most of us know that CPAs are conservative people. They are successful people and change is not easy for them, just like it is not easy for others in other professions, but CPAs have a responsibility to the public. They are next to physicians. They are the number one trusted business adviser; opportunities as well as responsibilities go along with that. I want to take the opportunity to focus on why I think people in our profession need to change, how they can change, and certainly they do not want to endanger themselves with risk, and why the methodology behind what we are talking about here has relatively small risk to them.

In fact the risk is greater if they do not change a little bit about the timing of that change, so they do it at the right time, not waiting too long or doing it too early. Then who must be involved in the change? Change is great. We all talk about it as individuals, but normally change is great as long as it is others that have to change. I am not the one that has to change, but in this case I think we all must change as a team and as a profession. Finally what is the price of the change? Generally to make the change you have to leave something behind, and there are certainly some things that as a profession we will probably leave behind, but to me it is far more exciting looking into the future, the new innovation and how technology really allows us to leverage those opportunities.

Susan: What is one of the most significant changes?

Gary: Historically CPAs and accountants have charged for their services by the hour. We call that the effort based economy where so many hours times X dollars is what the value of the service is, but today we are in a results based economy. Because technology has automated a lot of things, it has cut back the number of hours needed to do a job, while increasing the value of the service. The profession is being transformed from an hourly billing profession into one that is based upon the value being provided to the client. The big difference now is the client determines the value of the service not the number of hours you put into the project.

Susan: Accounting firms have primarily charged on an hourly basis. But now there is a push to move towards charging not by the hour but by the result, is that right?

Gary: Yes, I would say for the past 50 years accountants have charged using hours times dollars, but many of them are trying to change to a new model, just like the legal profession is also doing. To make that change, however, the firms have to have discussions upfront with their clients as to the scope of the service, and many of them are entering into what we call fixed price agreements or value price agreements. The big difference is it requires upfront conversations rather than waiting until the end of the project is done, calculating the hours times the dollars, and invoicing them what the price is going to be.

Susan: What is the advantage for the accounting firms of offering this new model?

Gary: The advantage to the accounting firms comes from the fact they are going to be able to compete in the marketplace, and they are going to be able to expand the type of services they offer. In the past they primarily offered tax and accounting services, or what we refer to as compliance based services. The growth in the accounting industry is happening with what is called advisory services. This is a big advantage to the accountant to be able to move into this new area for revenue growth. It is also advantageous to the client because the client will have a trusted advisor that can now offer far more services and higher level services than before when they primarily offered services just in the compliance arena. They are expanding their advisory services well beyond tax and accounting.

Susan: Accountants are shifting from a primarily compliance role to a more forward thinking, strategic advisory with their clients, is that what I heard you say?

Gary: Yes. That is definitely it. I often use the analogy of someone sitting upfront in a truck and looking out the front to the future versus someone sitting in the back of that truck and looking out as a historian and telling people where they have been and what they have done. While there is value to offering those services, and they are still very much needed, those compliance services have become commoditized as more and more people enter the profession and because we have better technology, the value for compliance services is driven down. With new technology to provide immediate real time information to clients, they want their advisor to deliver that information now and help them make decisions into the future rather than just decisions of the past.

For some organizations, they are not comfortable with this new role, but other firms are very comfortable, and I think part of what we are trying to do is transition the profession into becoming more comfortable in that role as a whole.

Susan: Because CPAs have been trained to look at historical data, you want to help CPAs to transition to where they can help their clients on where they are going, not just help them how they have done to date. It is a completely different perspective.

Gary: Absolutely, and the next generation of CPAs and accountants are trained to offer these different levels of services. What we have done is tried to simplify it for the CPA firm because often times when the world is becoming more complex, more regulated, more complicated for both the client and their advisor, you have to step back and simplify in order to break through the ceiling of the complexity. I should attribute that concept to Dan Sullivan who is the founder of the Strategic Coach Program. He has always said to go to the next level you have to evaluate where you are today, where you want to get to at the next level, and then define it in a simplified manner or plan.

More complexity is not going to allow you to get to that next level. It is only going to keep you from advancing, and that is what we are trying to do in this book is help them understand how they will be more successful, have more balance in their life, offer their clients more value, and really become more profitable going into the future.

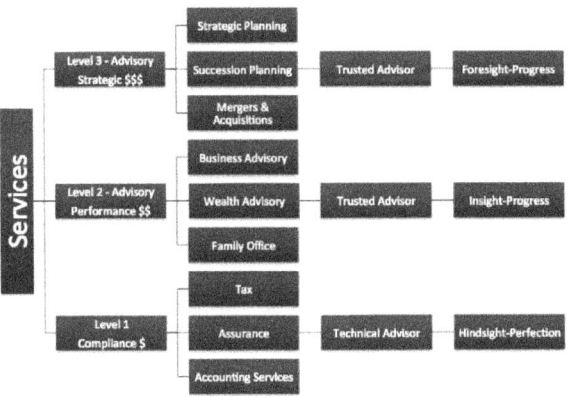

Susan: Do the CPA firms see this as the future for their organization? Do they not know how to migrate to these new services or is this kind of a new concept altogether?

Gary: It is totally a new concept. The technology that was necessary for collaboration among the CPA advisers and their clients has really come about through cloud based technology which is readily available today. In the past the only way we could manage this was to transfer files from one advisor to another or from the client to their advisor. Now with the cloud based technology, all advisers with proper security and access can operate all the same files. There is instantaneous information available to those advisers, and therefore their advice is timelier and more valuable to the small business owner.

Susan: The technology is the critical piece here because the technology of the past would not have allowed them to look out the front window, as you said, with their client because they would not have real time data to do so, is that right?

Gary: That is absolutely right. We have had an evolution in technology in this arena over the past 25 years, and probably one of the biggest revolutions came when Intuit invented Quick-Books. Prior to that time, most accounting and bookkeeping companies helped their clients do their books, but with the advent of the personal computer over 20 years, probably 25 years ago, and the initiation of Quick-Books and their initial formats, that allowed the small business person to bring much of that work in-house. There are advantages to having it in-house, but there are also disadvantages if you do not have the right skill sets for bookkeeping and for technology.

We are finding today that with cloud based systems, most small business people want to focus on growing their business, not on doing the back office work like accounting, bill payment, payroll, HR, those types of services. They would rather outsource those to someone who can do it better cheaper and easier. That is the role that the accounting firm can play today, being able to help the business do it faster, better, cheaper and easier, but when they do that they then have access to real time information. It allows them to provide much higher value services such as budgeting, cash flow, financing, and even if you want to take it to another level, and I will explain this little bit later, is take it to the strategic level, and that would be assisting the small business with their strategic plan, a succession plan, or even a technology plan because every business today is touched in some way by technology.

Susan: If you think about it, I cannot think of a person better suited to strategically help a business run than a CPA. They have the business expertise and now with technology they have real-time access to the data they need to help the business grow.

Gary: That is where this cloud based platform comes into play. Without the technology and the cloud, it was impossible to do that very efficiently. Therefore many accounting firms said we are just not going to do that business because we cannot offer it as cheaply or at a price that clients are willing to pay, so many of them got out of that business. I am not professing today to get back in that business because the platform is available. I am saying they need to get back in the business because the platform enables them to offer higher valued service based upon this foundation of having access to accurate and timely accounting information.

For example it is very difficult to do a cash-flow statement if you do not have accurate financial information for the prior year and be able to make some assumptions as to what the growth of your business is going to be. But if you have that information, it is almost, I hate to use this term, but push of the button to get a cash flow projection, but you have to have accurate historical information to do so, and as you say the CPA is sitting in the catbird seat really here with small business. That is what we are trying to get them to realize as well as instruct the marketing message to the small business clients that we are open for business in this area, and we can do it faster, better, cheaper than anyone else, but we can also do these higher level services that will help you grow your business and be of more value to you as a business person.

Susan: You want to help them make that transition from the traditional services that we have come to expect, but in addition to those services now add more forward thinking strategic services, advisory services. Is that correct?

Gary: Right I think the big differentiation here is that these services can be spread throughout the year so they are not compressed into a particular busy season and most accountants prior to April 15th are just so busy; they cannot do anything but the compliance work. If they have the right platform and the right services and relationships set up with their clients, they can virtually be doing everything but filing the returns throughout the year. Then when it is filing time, they know the information is accurate, and all they have to do then is run it through their calculation programs or taxes, and it speeds up that process and keeps them from having to work the number of hours of overtime that they do this time of year.

Susan: It is going to level the work load out for them.

Gary: Right. Some people have learned to live with that. They work very, very hard for a few months out of a year, and then they have a lifestyle where they do not have to work so hard, but most accounting firms, say the top 500 firms, are full time businesses. What they are doing and what they are challenged with is offering these services to their clients because the clients are requesting them, but it is finding the talent and the people that can offer this service on a timely basis. Again I go back to the technology; without the technology you cannot do it.

Relevance - Does Your Firm Have It?

Susan: You mentioned they need to have relevance for their service area. Why is that important, Gary?

Gary: I think everyone wants to remain relevant in their business. If you are not relevant, you are only going to see a decline, and you are going to see commoditization of your business. Someone will always do something cheaper. That does not mean that they will do it better, but they will do it cheaper. If you are going to remain relevant you have to listen to your clients. What is keeping your clients up at night? What are the opportunities that they really want to focus on, and how did they leverage their strengths?

I will tell you that most small business one of their dangers and concerns that keeps them up at night is all this accounting and regulation to make sure they are in compliance. They would prefer to source that to a company that has a unique process and that can do it at an affordable rate. That is where this platform comes in, but if I am an accounting firm and I can add additional services to that, say I could add strategic planning, say I could add budgeting, I could add even an insurance review for that client and package all those services together in one package. The value of that service becomes much higher to the small business than if I did it individually.

That small business person would prefer to go to the same supplier rather than have different suppliers for all facets of their business.

To simplify things we have broken services into three main levels:

Level 1 – Compliance

Level 2 – Performance

Level 3 – Strategic

Susan: Are the accounting firms embracing this change? Meaning, are they eager to offer these new types of services?

Gary: Embrace may be too strong a word. They are very interested in growing their businesses. They know they have to grow in order to be able to provide the services the clients are asking for. The challenge to them is that many think that if I select the right technology platform this will all happen. I think it is much more complex than that, and that they have to have a new pricing model for this. They have to be able to package and price their services. They have to have a delivery team to deliver, and they have to have processes that are very efficient. That is why we talk about the five Ps a lot in this. I will just touch on them quickly here, and then we will talk more about them in some of the future chapters.

Every firm needs a plan, and I would say if you do not have a one page plan, you probably are not going to be able to focus on what is important. You are just going to focus on what is up that day. You have to have a platform that we have been discussing a lot, and that is the technology. You have to have the right people and normally this is a unique ability team where everyone does not look like a 'Mini Me.' They have different skill sets. They work together well as a team, and they complement each other. You have to have the right pricing, and one of the biggest challenges with pricing is to determine what type of clients you are going to serve.

Are you going to serve clients that pay you a $1000 a year, $5000 a year, $20,000? You have to determine what league you want to play in, and then devise your pricing your services accordingly. Finally you have to cut out loops in the processes you utilize. You have to make those processes simple and use the principle of Six Sigma. You probably heard that from a manufacturing standpoint. It really applies to accounting firms as well. If you can reduce loops in the process and make sure your processes are efficient, then you drive errors in those processes out at a lower cost. In the accounting profession often times errors in processes have been driven out at the partner level or the highest level of cost.

That is why processes are so important in this overall strategy in order to cut your cost, get efficiency, and guarantee that you are not going to have a lot of errors or risk in the process.

Susan: There are a lot of pieces to this. It is not just a simple formula of now we are going to start offering these new services. It is almost like they have to be coached to think differently about their business. Is that true?

Gary: Absolutely. Most of us are trained to think about things or people. In this case, that is probably one of the biggest challenges is to think about how we think in order to be able to really understand the type of services that we want to offer and what the client is asking from us. It is a communication challenge to make sure we are on the same page with our clients. I think you hit the nail right on the head with regard to thinking in that often times we get in a group, and we generally bring our friends or people that are like us into that group. Therefore, we get what I would call directional innovation. In other words, we are all pointing in the same direction, so we kind of marginally improve upon something, but we really do not have what I would call true innovation.

If you have different people from different disciplines in that same room and you give them the same problem, chances are they will come up with something that is far more innovative because it is intersectional innovation rather than directional. I think the thinking part of this is of utmost importance because people naturally think about things, people, or thoughts, but if you think about your thinking process here and how you are going to approach this, I think it will make a critical difference in the direction that your firm heads in the future.

Susan: Because I think that they, as you said, think this is the future, I would think that the accounting firms would be eager for this only because this seems like this would be performing at their highest level with their clients. It is one thing to report on how the clients performed. It is a whole other game and a whole other level of strategic thinking to help them get to where they want to go. It is almost a cultural mind shift that the firms need to make.

The 10 X versus 2 X Approach

Gary: You are absolutely right. The challenge there is change the culture, change the game. If you want to change the results, you really have to change the thinking and the culture of people within that firm. The challenge for larger firms in particular is that you have people that are just entering the profession, and you have people that are baby boomer age who are leaving the profession. They are motivated in entirely different ways. True leaders have to lead both groups and build consensus and build some excitement over what is our strategy for the future, where is our firm headed. That is one reason that I think the byline here is very, very important; this requires 10 times thinking.

In his book *Great by Choice,* Jim Collins pointed out that if you want to have people follow you and particularly talented people follow, you having a 10 times approach is much more exciting and provides a lot more opportunity than the approach we are going to grow incrementally 7% to 10% a year. Anybody can say we are going to grow 7% to 10% a year, but when I say we have a 10 times strategy people are going to say, "Well there is something in it for me then." How you do that, and how you get everybody pulling in the same direction is the challenge here.

Susan: When you say 10 times growth, you mean the accounting firm that does $3 million a year can go to $30 million? Is that what you mean?

Gary: They could be a $30 million firm, and you have jumped to a conclusion most people jump to. Ten times does not necessarily only apply to revenue. What if we improved our turnaround time on projects by 10 times? In other words if it takes 14 days to get a tax return out, what if we get improve that ten times and get it down to one and half days? What if we could improve the customer experience in the firm? Those are all things that I think have meaning with regard to 10 times, but most people get caught in this, well if I am a $3 million firm I am going to be a $30 million firm, but I can even take the metrics of that $3 million firm and tell you that if you are a $3 million firm 80% of your revenues are produced by 20% of your clients.

If in that $3 million firm you had $15,000 as an average client and pick whatever you want and the firms will pick an amount that maybe high, maybe low, but if you just divided $3 million by $15,000 that means they have 200 clients. There is a good chance that 20% of those 200 clients or 40 of those clients are producing 80% of the revenue or $2.4 million. Now when I divide that $2.4 million by 40 clients, that means the revenue per client is $60,000 a person. What if I instead had 40 could grow that 10 times to 400 clients at 60,000; I am at $24 million. You see if we focus on the right clients and the right service, we will be far more profitable with more satisfied clients, and be able to offer our employees a balanced work environment rather than try to do everything for everyone and have them frustrated and unfocused and not growing.

This is the real challenge. Until you break those numbers down, sometimes you do not really see how easy it would be if you were just focused on the right clients. You are spending way too much time on people that may only pay you a $1000 a year and you are doing one thing for them, maybe a 1040. Well that is a $1000, but you could be taking care of better clients and providing not only that tax return but a lot of other services for those clients that wanted.

Susan: You are actually challenging these firms to think differently about their business model and view it from a much larger point of view. Asking them to ask themselves: How can they leverage the shift in the market rather than stay with the same revenue model? You are suggesting the game has changed, therefore they have to change.

Gary: Right, and I am not being critical in any way of many of these firms because many of them started out in a time where they really felt like they had to take any work that came in the door, and they get to a certain level, and then that work consumes all of their capacity, but it does not pay very well. What I am saying is that to get to that next level you have to think differently, and you have to have a different economic model than you do when you are starting the firm.

Susan: Very well said. With that in mind then, you want to help them learn how to make that shift via this book. You are going to share all of the elements they need to take into account if they want the growth.

Gary: That is right. They have to want to do this, and it is going to force some change upon them. There is a good friend of mine, Alan Coltan, that always says there are three doors you can enter through. Door #1 is the door that we know we need to change, but we are doing pretty well we just do not want to change, and for some people that is fine but do not tell yourself you are going to change. Just say you are going to go through door #1 and continue doing what you have been doing. Door#2 is we know we need to change. We are going to make some changes, but everybody else is going to make the change. I am not going to make the change.

Then door#3 is we are going to have to make some changes, and we are all going to have to have skin in the game and buy in; we are going to have to make some tough decisions. If the firm decides to change and certain individuals or people do not want to participate in that change, we are going to have to some terminations and rebuilding the teams, and we are going to have to make some tough decisions. That is where a lot of firms are today. They are realizing that, and now they are making some tough decisions. The platform to allow them to do that has been in the making for several years and is available to them today. That is one thing that I think is encouraging and why I am excited to write about this.

The Five Ps

The Plan

Susan: For the firm that says we are on board. We want this. We want to start offering higher levels of services, but we do not really know where to begin, can you walk us through how to begin?

Gary: Let's start with the Five Ps. These are the critical areas that if they do not address these five, the chance of their success goes down immensely. While I say they cannot because eventually they figure it out, but if you kind of have a road map to start with, you do not have to go down the dead ends. You do not have to make a lot of turns. You can pretty much do a straight line.

The first P that I say is you have to a plan, and many people said the planning process is more important than the plan. I will say there is a lot of truth to that statement especially in a professional service organization where you have multiple people in leadership positions, and if they are not on the same page, it is going to be difficult to lead your people in a shared vision rather than a shared service company.

What we recommend is that they develop a road map and one that allows them to focus on the big rocks and ignore the meaningless interruptions that distract e.g., the sand. It is awfully easy to have a plan, but when sand comes in you want to put that in your bucket, and you really ought to put the big rocks in your bucket first and then fill it up full of sand. I think Cuffy was the one that demonstrated that, at least that was the first time I ever saw it. We have the model in our company, "Think, plan, and grow." As we alluded to earlier you have to spend some time in thinking and planning, but I have grown up in this profession, and I know there is not a lot of time for thinking and planning.

The profession tends to be active because when they are in action, they get the bill time. We have designed a planning methodology that allows them to put together a one page strategic plan that identifies their strategic objectives, their measurements of success. It is great to have objectives, but if you do not have any way to measure them, then you really do not know whether you have been successful at the end. Dollars and profits are really a result. Yes it is a measurement, but that is not the only measurement. Is your firm sustainable, will there be another generation of owners? Will it continue to offer high quality service to your clients? Those are also measurements.

Then you have to come up with the priorities that the firm wants to initiate. What are the due dates on the responsible parties on those, so you hold people accountable? That really allows the firm to leverage their internal resources as well as any external resources they have access to. What do I mean by external resources? That could be they could source out some of this work to other entities in our profession. It gets as wild as we are going to do this in India or another country, although that tends to be coming back more to the US with the technology that is available today.

Even more important than this plan is the accountability and execution because it is not that difficult to put the plan together, but it is difficult for people to make sure that it gets executed. That is the first P, and one that in the book we will give an example. We find that if you have an example, it is much easier to do than if you just give that one page plan with a lot of instructions. If it is different, you will change it.

Susan: Gary is this plan for the accounting firm to use for themselves, or is this the plan that they will use for their future client that they want to now go after?

Gary: This is the plan they will use for themselves, but as part of that plan they need to target their clients. You are really thinking ahead because if I am going to go to this advisory service, I am not just out looking for individual income tax work, or I am not just out probably looking for audits. I am going for more advisory services in addition to tax work. To give you a good example, we know of firms across the country that have given up $10,000 of audits to do $120,000 of advisory services for the same clients. We are seeing a lot more of that today as governmental entities and other business outsource their back office.

Susan: It is interesting that companies are moving toward outsourcing when you think the technology would actually provide the opposite for them.

Gary: It provides collaboration. If I can source a part time CFO, or if I can source an HR person or an IT person for part time, rather than bringing them into my small business, and you have to remember an awful lot of small businesses are under $10 million, in fact a lot of them are $3 million. They cannot really afford those kind of services on a full time basis, but if they can spend x thousand dollars a month and have access to that expertise as much as they need when they need it, and it is all done through collaboration, it makes a lot of sense. Sourcing or meshing - lady by the name of Lisa Gansky came up with the term the Mesh and has written a book about it.

There are several examples in the world today without an internet based platform you could not mesh. One of the best ones that I think is Vacation Rental by Owner. You can go out there, you can see videos, you can get user reviews, anything you want, and it is because of that internet platform. Another one is Rate My Professor, and there is even one out now, Rate my Accountant. The transparency level goes up as the service has to go up. That is just part of the world that we are working in today.

Susan: Tying this back to the plan that the firm needs to sit down and do some strategic thinking about their plan and how they go about doing that plan is what you are addressing here.

Gary: Right.

The Platform

Susan: Let's talk about this platform that you keep alluding to. Is the platform different than the internet?

Gary: The internet is part of the platform, and the platform from an accountant's perspective maybe not be in the small businessman's perspective, but the central core or engine is based upon accounting. Then around that economic engine would be what we call the ecosystem, and that ecosystem may have software applications that are developed by the developer of the accounting system, or they could be developed by other developers, but they all fit together and work together much like Legos do. Let me give you an example of that.

We have the accounting engine here that could be something like Quick-Books online, Intacct or a company called Zero, but to pay bills the company would use a program like bill.com. Bill.com has taken the bill payment process and cut the time by over 50%. The company looks a lot more professional when they handle their bills. When the bills come in, they simply send them to bill.com. The documents are all stored, and then there is work flow and the process that allows multiple levels of management or a single level of management if it is a real small company to approve and pay those bills.

The bills are paid electronically or by check, and the company does not have to write or sign the check. That is all done through the banking system. You can turn that around and do it now for accounts receivable and eventually will cut the credit cards out of accounts receivable, so you do not have to pay 2% or 3% of account receivables. By having this type of platform, and that can go on way beyond those examples because there a whole lot of others, it allows you operate very efficiently on a timely basis and have integration of all this information so that you do not have to have multiple databases with the same data in multiple locations e.g., the customer name, cellphone number. It is maintained in one location.

I can also add on to that ecosystem something like a CRM package to manage my growth. I can add on work flow. I can add on scheduling, and these things all fit together, and that is why this platform is so important. Most of the vendors now are finding out that the accountants are the ones that really are in the catbird seat here and that they are selling through the accounting profession to the small business client saying you need your accountant involved in this in order to make all this work together. There is something in it for the vendor, there is something in it for the small business person, and there is something in it for the accountant.

With collaboration the value of the service continues to increase, but platform is the differentiator that allows you to really compete in this environment. I guess the last thing I would say about platform is there are a lot of different definitions of being in the cloud, and some people are trying to say that we can emulate cloud based services and still use client base services in the cloud and that will suffice, but for the long term this really has to be web based applications in my opinion to get the full value of the entire system.

Susan: Do they already have this platform in place, or is it a new thing that they are going to have to go out and source to be providing these different types of service for their clients?

Gary: Most of them do not have the platform in place, and they have been focusing on their own internal technology which would be the preparation of tax returns, the preparation of financial statements, and their time and billing systems. That is internal technology. That, too, is moving to the cloud, and as they move that to the cloud they start to see the opportunities for using other cloud based software, not only in their own practices but for their clients. You can probably motivate a firm to move faster if there is revenue opportunity in it for clients than if it is just for their own internal benefit. The real leaders out there are trying to move as quickly as possible because it cuts down on the infrastructure that firms have to have.

It allows them to have consistency among locations. It allows them to have a remote workforce, a workforce that works from home. It allows them to have hardware agnostic systems, and by that I mean I can run this on an Apple; I can run it on a windows based PC; I can run it on a tablet. I can run it on an iPhone. You may wonder why anyone would want to do their business books on an iPhone. I know a lot of MacDonald franchises with owners that will look at their iPhone and see their sales record for the day. That is more valuable to them than seeing a monthly profit and loss at the end of the month because they already know that is going to be approximately through the real time sales information

They also like to watch their cash flow, how much cash they have in their bank. This platform is very critical to firms being able to move to the next level of advisory services in my mind.

Susan: If the relationship with their client is going to be a lot more collaborative, they need to have the technology in place which supports that collaboration.

Gary: Right. You cannot really do this halfway. We see some firms that have kind of figured it out, but we see they are doing this randomly. What we are trying to do is develop their processes to the point that it is no longer random. It is their unique process, and they are doing it efficiently and therefore it is scalable. It is not just that one legged individuals could do this. If they could take a team of people and train them, they could do it.

The People

Susan: The next P is the People. I have to imagine that this has got to be one of the pieces for them to have to have a strategic plan on.

Gary: Absolutely, and it is one that our profession has not done as good a job of investing in the people coming up as we probably could have. We are fortunate in that we have a lot of people in accounting education today in the US, and those numbers are up because the AICPA and many of the large firms saw those numbers declining. Accounting has been a stable job. It has been a relatively good starting salary. It has been a good place to learn. If you wanted to go into other business professions, having an accounting degree has been good. Now the challenge going forward is we just do not have enough of those people to replace the baby boomers that are leaving, so how are we going to do more with less people, and how are we going to use our systems to really pick up the slack is the question.

The Delivery Team Approach

That is why people are so important, and Jim Collins has said you have to get the right people on the bus, the wrong people off the bus. I would say that is true for our profession and that comes with the planning process. Then even more important, you have to get people in the right seat on the bus. They may be on the right bus, but too often you have them in a position that does not really utilize their unique ability. There are several testing methodologies that have a lot of validity to them. Strength finders is one. The Kolbe Index is another. Using these tools to help the firm not only recruit and retain people in the right position is instrumental, but also having programs that develop more than just technical skills, they develop the leadership skills as well. That is very, very important today.

Firms were investing heavily in the middle, trying to get people ready to become partners in these firms as the baby boomers retire. That is one of the reasons in my mind that we have seen so many mergers. One, firms want to grow, and two, they are trying to acquire talent in the process. Talent is very important, and I think any company that can develop talent, even if they develop more talent than they need, will be highly successful because they are already going to have a supply. If you develop talent, you will get to keep the best talent. That is why I have them listed in an order. I do not try to prioritize because that would be kind of silly. You have to have all of these things.

Susan: With some of these new skills that are required, do they have to retrain their current employees? This is a whole new business model that they are actually going to be going after. To those individuals who are going to have to help deliver those services they will need new and different skills they do not currently have access to, yes?

The Processes

Gary: Yes, that is where the next P comes in, Processes. In other words, you have to train people to the processes that you are going to utilize. Some of the processes in the past had been focused on aggregation of data. Think of your own personal tax return. One of the things you have paid for in the past is to have your local CPA aggregate a lot of that data in order to put it on the form. Over the past few years now much of that data that they aggregate is already in digital form: your bank, your brokerage house, anybody paying you interest or dividends.

So that aggregation process has now been automated, and it does not take nearly as long to aggregate it if they have the right processes in place. If they are still using the processes they were five years ago, chances are they have got a lot of loops and inefficiencies in those processes. That is why people have to be trained, and technology is rapidly changing. Think of the iPad. Three or four years ago there was no iPad. I think it will be four years this April. It has virtually revolutionized how people operate and get content as has the iPhone. These changes are rapid, and they require training, and often times we think people will just figure it out. That is pretty inefficient.

Anybody that has an iPhone, if somebody gave them an hour's training on it, would save then probably several hours of time of just trying to figure it out.

The Pricing - Pick a Number, Any Number!

Susan: How do you recommend they address pricing?

Gary: I often say pick a number, and that is the number that I want to put in to your league. We will offer in this book a pricing matrix sample. There have been very good books written on pricing strategy. Ron Baker has written several of those. I agree with his strategy towards pricing, pricing on value rather than pricing on time, but I think what we have found in this area is the first thing the firm has to deal with are what size of clients do they really want to target? There is always an outlier and everyone wants to think about the client that is going to say pay them $200,000, or the one that is going to pay them $500,000 a year.

That is probably not the client you want to target. It may be a client that is going to pay you $20,000 a year. You kind of get in the ballpark with the pricing matrix of what services could you offer for that $20,000, and what services could you add to take them to a higher level, or what services could they subtract to take them to a lower level. In doing so, you develop a matrix, and you sit down with the client and have a discussion early on. Think of this as a menu much like you would have in a restaurant where you would have items that come from the compliance level, you would have items that come from the performance level of the firm, and you would have items that come from the strategic level.

Let me give you examples of items from all three levels, so you can understand what I am talking about. In the compliance level, you may have a small corporation in this business, so you might have a sub chapter s corporation with some states that you need to file. You might also have a personal income tax return that you need to file. Those would be compliance items. I could add several others like a monthly or quarterly compiled financial statement if I wanted to adjust that area. I am not going to for today's example; I am going to take you onto what we call level three or performance. That would be if you want to know how you are doing compared to other businesses.

Let's say you are in the landscape business; you would like to know how you compare to other landscapers across the country. In order to get those metrics and do a comparison, we call that level two or performance. Another performance level two item might be how you get additional financing for growth. One could be a cash flow statement; one could be just simple as a budget. Sometimes these are referred to CFO type advisory services. Then I am going to take you to the third level which we call strategic services or strategic plan; a succession plan would be another example.

I may have up to 50 or 100 items spread among those three level of services, but I sit down with you and walk you through the menu of services, and you simply check which ones you would be interested in. Now as we get down to what the total cost is you may say, "Well I just do not think I can afford to do that," or "I feel I can afford to do that this year," so you eliminate that. Then let's say that bundle of services amounts to $20,000. In the past, most firms would have done the work and then billed for the services they completed.

In today's environment we would recommend asking the client for a commitment of 15 to 20% paid upfront and then a monthly fee for the balance over the next 12 months. At the end of the 12 months, we go through that menu of services again and look at the pricing, and we would know whether they had exceeded that, or if they had not used everything, and we would know that could also use an adjustment. We also have a change order clause in that contract, so that if something happens and they acquire another business and they want more service, we could add to that.

You can start to see where these discussions change based on people's needs and the firm's ability to deliver, and that way there is some protection in the agreement for all parties.

Susan: The firm will have to educate their clients on the benefits of what these new services are, so it is kind of like a whole dialogue that goes on between the firm and their clients that they have not been having in the past.

Gary: Precisely, and it needs to be a dialogue. I could take you through that scenario I just talked about. I could tell you that you could hire somebody that could probably do your tax returns, do your financial statement, but a bookkeeper for a small business is going to cost $50,000 a year or more, and you would be very lucky if you could get a part timer. Then as they leave, you have to struggle to hire somebody that you really do not know much about. You also have to manage them. It just makes a whole lot more sense for you to contract with your accounting firm and have them do that for you.

Susan: I would think when you do that it is a more holistic approach. This way the small business owner does not have to have one firm do service X and another do service Y. If your CPA firm handles everything for you, that has got to be easier for the business owner.

Gary: Plus they can kind of budget. They know what the cost is going to be, and there are not a lot of surprises, and they also may not have to go hire as many people. If their company is growing rapidly, it allows them to use the resources of the accounting firm. Also they do not have to invest heavily in technology in the platform we are talking about because everything is backed up to the cloud. If they add another 20 employees to the payroll, that is a minimal pay. They do not have to get a lot more technology to do that. It is just a very scalable business model that they have control of.

Susan: What else can you share with us on the Five Ps?

Gary: We have kind of touched of processes a little bit, but we should probably talk a little bit about why process is so important. I touched on

Six Sigma, and most people feel that Six Sigma really applies to engineering, not so much to accounting firms, but as you bring this technology in, you can cut out a lot of steps in your process, and by those steps we have always had the review process, and we have always tracked data to the source documents in most firms. With a technology system that brings that information in from the original source documents, we can eliminate a lot of those steps and save a lot of costs.

From a sales standpoint, if I have a process, and I have named that process and drawn a diagram of the process, and I show the client our process, it could be the Boomer Process whatever it is. If I show the client that it has a name on it, I own that process, the client is going to say these guys have thought this through, and they are more efficient than I am. They are probably more efficient than the competition down the street. It helps to have these processes identified. It also helps if you are going to scale this across multiple offices or if you are going to scale it to a large number of clients because you get consistency, and you also make yourself much more efficient.

Process is very, very important, and it is one of the things that often times accountants and even small businesses think that they will just define themselves, but they do not. It takes somebody that really understands the details and how to make it work.

Susan: It is not enough for the accounting firm to just come up with the solution for the clients. You are saying go ahead and label the service. Name it something. Trademark it, so it has more intrinsic value for the client, but it also then becomes more of the standard of practice?

Gary: Yes, if I can name that process it is much easier to market. It is much easier for the client to see value, and therefore it all starts to fit together. We have multiple services that we offer our clients, and to give an example, we call that the Boomer Advantage. There are various services under the Boomer Advantage. We have defined processes under that overall process, so that our clients can see how we are more efficient at this than say our competitors. They also start taking those names and identifying with us rather than just think it is generic.

The Importance of a Peer Network

Susan: Have you worked with other companies to make this transition from doing the traditional level one service to offering level three type services?

Gary: Yes, we have worked with companies in a couple of ways. With one company, we have done one-on-one consulting with them to help them develop their plan, select their platform, develop their team etc., worked on The Five Ps. We also have a community called The Producer Circle that involves several of the best firms in the country who are doing this. We feel that from a peer community you get access to expertise access to your peers and personal development that you will not get if you just try to figure it out on your own. The Producer Circle meets twice a year, and there are generally 20 to 25 firms in that.

We are also doing something new this year. We are inviting some of the key platform players, so that you have exposure to their training methodology. You have an understanding of how they fit in the ecosystem of this platform, and we have asked them to be more than just sponsors or vendors. We have asked them to actually participate in the program. We think this community knowledge and having access to peers as well as expertise that you would not in your own firm is very important to speed up your growth. It provides confidence, new capabilities, and I guess it is all of the things that values created by its leadership that provides direction, relationship provides confidence and creativity provides new capabilities. That is all wound in to this community.

Susan: Is this peer group made up of your clients?

Gary: These are for Boomer consulting clients who are in this peer group, and we facilitate it for them.

Susan: You meet twice a year, and do you meet outside of that time frame?

Gary: They also have access to us on an ongoing basis. We feel there is still value in face-to-face meetings and personal relationships, but we also appreciate the capabilities of videos and webinars, so we get try to get them together at least on a quarterly basis in addition to the two times that they meet in person.

Here's Your Roadmap to Transform and Grow Your Accounting Firm

Susan: For the accounting firm that embraces this concept and wants to get started but does not quite know where to start, what do you recommend that they do?

Gary: There are two options from our perspective. One is they can hire someone like us as a consultant to come in and work with them one-on-one, and I would say sometimes that is a better alternative than peer-to-peer. If they have already started doing it and have kind of figured out it, then peer-to-peer might be the best direction. What we find is most firms know what they need to do to make the change, but they have multiple opinions as to how they are to get there. It takes somebody from the outside to provide the facilitation, the guidance, and the expertise to get it, so that it will go through the organization in an organized fashion.

One of the ways to say you really support something but you do not is to say we are going to support it and then procrastinate and nothing ever happens. That is one of the things that is going to happen in an accounting firm. Everyone says yes, but it is always somebody else's responsibility, and we try to avoid making those types of critical mistakes.

Susan: They could bring your company in to provide that outside influence they need to effect change. Managers do not always embrace change even though they say they do.

Gary: I think it is the accountability factor. If you have parties from all different perspectives that are servicing the clients, it is almost like a directional versus intersectional innovation. You get a better perspective, and you get the best result for the client that is offering the value. It really takes the personal perspective out of it. Not that personal perspective is bad, but it can be biased because you only see part of the situation. We are trying to really add value here to support the small business because that keeps the firm relevant and makes them more successful for the long term.

Susan: How can someone reach you with questions?

Gary: Well a couple of ways. I will certainly give you my office number which is 785-537-2358. Our website is www.boomer.com, and my email address is lgboomer@boomer.com.

Susan: There is a lot to consider here, isn't there Gary? It is not a case of we are going to start offering this new type of service, but these firms actually have to take a very strategic approach to it. They cannot just add to their current workload and hope it will work out.

Gary: Right because if they try to add without taking something off, it will not happen. At least it will not happen with the degree of success they anticipate.

Susan: If it is not handled right, the people that deliver the service it will just see it as, "Ah more work," instead of having that cultural shift of, "Hey let's make this exciting." They have to get everyone on board with this for it to be a true success. That is not easily done. That is not going to happen with just a memo from a Vice President.

Gary: Right, you cannot do this in a memo. That is why you need a one page plan, and you need people to participate in that planning process that are for and against it. It is not just getting the cheerleaders involved. It is getting people that will question, and once they understand the why that is the emotional answer to their question then they become detailed and want to know the specifics of how they are going to get it done.

Susan: Thank you for sharing this with us today. It has been very enlightening, and I think it is exciting to think accounting firms will be able to provide these higher level of services going forward. I think that is very exciting.

Gary: It is, and the accounting firm can really help with the growth process and assist them in scaling their company up without having to go invest in a full time HR person, invest in a full time CFO or even an IT person. They can mesh or source those resources.

Susan: I never would have thought that my CPA firm could be a one stop solution for a lot of issues and challenges, but you are suggesting that is the future for these accounting firms and is in fact in place today.

Appendix: The Right Tools

Susan: Can you describe for us the items that are in the appendix, the tools that are available for these accounting firms. Can you describe what they are?

Gary: Sure I would be happy to. The purpose of the appendix items is to really give you the meat of the book here in a format that you can go out and use. You can change, and if we were to write about each one of these we would have 250 pages at least. We have shortened it. I am just going to go through quickly and tell you little about each one of the items. The getting started checklist is 10 questions, and you can use that as a checklist to get started and see how far along you are in this process. If you have not done anything, you probably can certainly get started with just the items that are here in book, but there are also ways that you can speed up that process.

The second item is a sample menu of services that lays your services that you may offer today out in level one, two, and three, and you will understand that better after you have gone through and looked at this, but it helps you have a discussion with clients and sit down upfront and determine what services they might like. For example you will notice that if there are a lot of services that you offer today that are not there, it is probably that there are some there that you do not offer, and you should think about them. That was part of the design process. There is no way we could include everything.

Then I want to have you look at 10 major differentiators between this new role as a trusted advisor and the role as a compliance or technical advisor. Just to give you one example this is more of a team sport whereas compliance was more of the rugged individualist. There are nine others that differentiate how you should think about this. Then there are questions in about I believe it is nine different areas that you can ask the clients, and this will prompt them to think and probably have them ask you questions about how you can assist them in these areas. This can range from something about their governance to their technology to their training and human resources.

You would not use all the questions at any time, but you might take questions from a section, and that would initiate a conversation you could have regarding that section with a client. I think it is a good starting point for you to use. The next is probably one of the most important, and this is pricing matrix. When you first said you wonder why we use the criteria that we did, I will tell you it really does not matter what criteria you use. It is more important that you know what ballpark you are wanting to play in and get a good understanding of what some of the services you can include for certain levels, and you will modify this as you go but it is a good starting point.

Finally is the one page plan. This is the document that shows the objectives. It shows measurements of success, initiatives, due dates, and who is responsible. I think if you have these items in the appendix along with the contents of the book, you should be able to have a good discussion in your firm to get started.

Susan: Thank you for the Appendix overview, Gary, and thank you for sharing your expertise with us today. This has been very enlightening.

Gary: My pleasure, Susan. Glad it was of value. We are passionate about helping accounting firms transform their business by offering higher level services to their clients, and anything I can do to assist in that is my pleasure.

Getting Started Checklist

☐ Do you know clients and potential clients who would benefit from performance and advisory services?

☐ Do you have a designated leader(s)?

☐ Are performance and advisory services part of the firm's strategic plan?

☐ Do you have a one-page advisory services strategic game plan?

☐ Do you have a budget and cash flow projection?

☐ Do you have a project manager(s)?

☐ Do you have a menu of services?

☐ Do you have a pricing strategy and related matrix that corresponds with the menu of services for target clients?

☐ Do you have a delivery platform and related ecosystem to insure accurate and real time information accessible from mobile devices?

☐ Do you have a unique ability delivery team?

☐ Do you have your unique processes defined and graphically illustrated?

☐ Are your processes scalable?

☐ Have you defined client responsibilities and training requirements?

☐ Do you have a sales plan?

☐ Do you belong to a peer network of firms who offer similar services?

Menu of Services

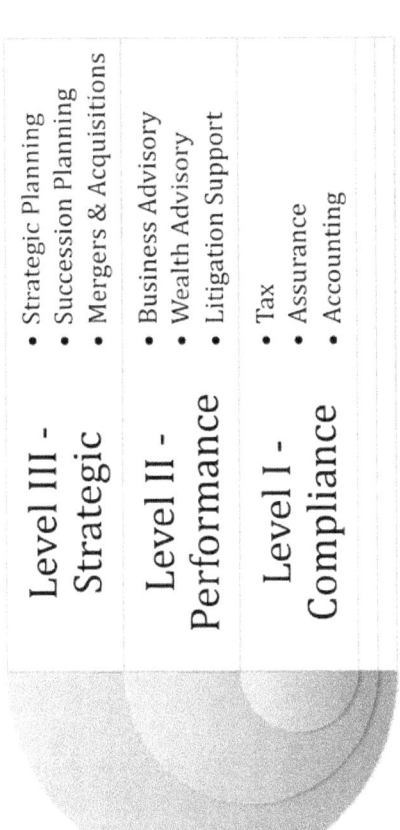

Sample Menu of Services

Level III - Strategic
- Strategic Planning
- Succession Planning
- Mergers & Acquisitions

Level II - Performance
- Business Advisory
- Wealth Advisory
- Litigation Support

Level I - Compliance
- Tax
- Assurance
- Accounting

The above list is for illustration purposes only. You should include other services you currently offer or plan to offer.

Sample Menu of Services

| | Advisory | |
Level 1 – Compliance	Level II – Performance	Level III - Strategic
Tax	**Business Advisory Services**	**Planning**
Planning	Budgeting	Strategic Planning
Compliance	Cash Flow	Succession Planning
Audit & Client Representation	Financing	Technology Review/Planning
State and Local Sales Tax	Business Analytics	90 Day Game Plans
Payroll Tax Compliance	Peer Metrics	Accountability Reviews
International Tax		Annual Plan Updates
	Wealth Advisory	
Assurance Services	Family Office	**Mergers and Acquisitions**
Compilation	Insurance Evaluation	
Review	Property & Casualty	
Audit	Life	
	Disability	
Accounting Services		
General Ledger & Reporting	**Litigation Support**	
Payroll		
Accounts Payable – Bill Payment	**Human Resources**	
Accounts Receivable	Performance Evaluation	
Expense Reporting	Training	
	Team Synergy	
	Business Valuation	

The above list is for illustration purposes only. You should include other services you currently offer or plan to offer.

10 Major Differentiators

Major Differentiators Among Services	
Level 1 - Compliance	**Level 2/3 – Advisory (Performance/Strategic)**
Rugged Individual	Team Sport
Seasonal	Non-Seasonal
Hourly Billing – After-The-Fact	Value Billing – Value Price Agreement
Reactive	Proactive
Based on Hindsight	Based on Insight and Foresight
Post Mortem	Planning – Strategic
Reporting - Historical	Anticipating and Predicting – Future Focused
Focus on Details	Focus on the Big Picture
Deliver a Product	Support a Process or Processes
Work with Accounting Personnel	Work with Leadership/Ownership

Advisory Services Pricing Matrix

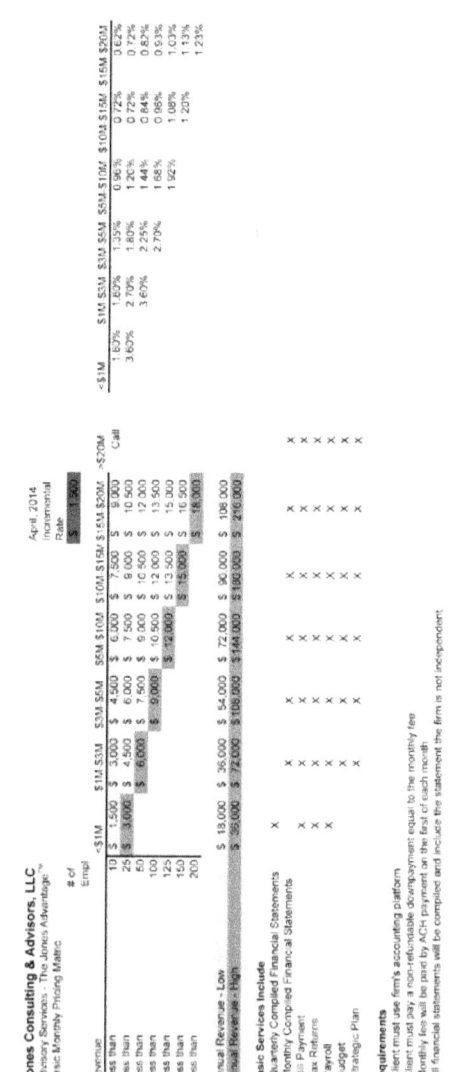

The Performance Management Questionnaire

Boomer Consulting, Inc.
The Performance Management Questionnaire

Page 1 of 2

	Comments

Leadership and Management

1. Does your company have a current strategic plan?
2. What are the ages of your senior management team?
3. Do you have a written exit/succession plan for all members of your management team?
4. Have you identified your replacement?
5. If so, who and what are you doing to develop that person?

Governance

1. What type of entity is the company?
2. Who is your legal counsel?
3. Are your agreements current and properly reflect the vision and mission of the company? (Stockholder, Buy-Sell, Leases & etc.)
4. Do you have external members on the Board of Directors or utilize an external Advisory Board?
5. Do you encourage selected clients/customers to participate in strategic planning?

Financial

1. Is your business as profitable as you would like?
2. What would be an acceptable profit level? $ _____ %
3. Do you receive accurate financial information on a timely basis?
4. What information would you like to receive that you currently are not receiving and would you like mobile capabilities?
5. Who is responsible for financial reporting?

Talent Development

1. Who is in charge of talent development?
2. Do you have an internal leadership program?
3. Do you have a training curriculum?
4. Do you utilize Project Managers and/or Administrative Assistants?
5. What is your rate of turnover?

Caution: The purpose of The Performance Management Questionnaire is to create conversations about the client or potential client and their business. It is not a checklist and every question does not need to be ask during a conversation. One of the best ways to utilize the questionnaire is to simply ask the client what is keeping him/her up at night and what they feel are their best opportunities. Based on their answers, you can go to the appropriate section or sections of the questionnaire.

57

Boomer Consulting, Inc.
The Performance Management Questionnaire

	Comments
Technology & Process Improvement	
1. Do you have a written IT plan and budget than integrates with your strategic plan?	
2. Who is responsible for IT and are your processes defined and documented?	
3. Have you had an external review of your technology management and infrastructure?	
4. Is you website an asset or a liability and do you have a social media strategy?	
5. Do you source your accounting and CFO responsibilities?	
Incentive Compensation	
1. Are your employees paid at or above market?	
2. Do you have a bonus or incentive structure in place?	
3. How often do you conduction salary adjustments?	
4. Is compensation tied to performance reviews?	
5. Is your compensation system closed or open?	
Client/Customer Development	
1. Have you provided internal Five Star customer service training?	
2. Have you conducted a client/customer satisfaction survey – Net Promoter?	
3. Have you conducted a pricing study?	
4. Do you have a customer loyalty program?	
5. Do you have a customer referral program?	
Brand and Market Share	
1. What is your market and brand exposure?	
2. Who is responsible for marketing and what is your budget?	
3. Would you like to expand your market? (Regional, National or International)	
4. Who manages business development and sales?	
5. Has your sales force been adequately trained?	
Personal	
1. Do you get and take adequate vacation time?	
2. Does the company have a sabbatical program for its leadership team?	
3. What are your personal goals? (1-5-10-20-lifetime)	
4. Do you have a personal coach?	
5. Do you participate in a peer network?	

Caution: The purpose of The Performance Management Questionnaire is to create conversations about the client or potential client and their business. It is not a checklist and every question does not need to be ask during a conversation. One of the best ways to utilize the questionnaire is to simply ask the client what is keeping him/her up at night and what they feel are their best opportunities. Based on their answers, you can go to the appropriate section or sections of the questionnaire.

Jones Consulting Strategic Plan

BOOMER
CONSULTING INC.

Jones Consulting & Advisors, LLC

2014 Strategic Game Plan – Advisory Services

Vision

To be the leader in our market offering compliance, performance and advisory services to businesses and their owners.

Core Values

- Trusted relationships
- Integrity
- Innovation
- Development and growth
- Respect and teamwork
- Accountability

Mission Statement

Jones leads clients to increased performance and profitability by providing performance and unique advisory services.

Strategic Objectives

- Enhance the firm's culture through corporate and personal development.
- Grow our performance and consulting services to exceed compliance revenues.
- Innovate around new and existing service opportunities.
- Improve, simplify and standardize processes and technology solutions.

Jones Consulting & Advisors – Advisory Services Game Plan – 2014

Strategic Objective	Measurement	Strategy/Initiative	Due Date	Assigned To
1. Enhance the firm's culture through corporate and personal development.	• Completion of Kolbe Index on all team members. • Completion of Quarterly Game Plans	1.1 Identify team resource requirements for Performance and Advisory services. 1.2 Create Personal Career Development plans for each team member. 1.3 Utilize the Kolbe Index & Synergy Reports in the development of unique ability teams. 1.4 Utilize quarterly game plan forms and incorporate think (future), plan (this quarter) and grow (learning) in the plan. 1.5 Give back to our community with an annual event. 1.6 Insure we schedule at least one team social event annually. 1.7 Schedule monthly lunch and learn roundtables to discuss service offerings.		
2. Grow our performance and consulting services to exceed compliance service revenues.	• Revenue growth from Performance & Advisory Services. • Number of new clients over $20k per year.	2.1 Identify leaders for the Performance and Advisory Service Segments 2.2 Develop and publish a menu of performance and advisory services that can be packaged with existing compliance services. 2.3 Develop the pricing strategy for target clients along with a related pricing matrix. 2.4 Build relationships and develop leads through New Opportunities calls and periodic client contact campaigns. 2.5 Develop related marketing materials and web site.		
3. Innovate around new & existing services.	• Completion of VPA • # of client conversations completed.	3.1 Conduct client conversations with the top 10% of clients regarding key performance and advisory services. Utilize the Performance Management Questionnaire as appropriate. 3.2 Define and document delivery processes and client responsibilities. 3.3 Create client videos for training and processes. 3.4 Approve a standard consulting and advisory services agreement with regard to scope, responsibilities, terms and deliverables. Include a change order clause		
4. Improve, simplify and standardize processes and technology solutions.	• Implementation of the Platform. • Implementation of Ecosystem applications • Measurement of defined processes	5.1 Implement a Cloud based Platform and ecosystem that will meet the needs of the majority of our clients and targeted prospects. Initial considerations are: • Accounting – Payroll – Bill Payment – Expense Reporting • Receivables/Cash Flow - Document Management – Workflow • Project Management - Business Analytics – CRM 5.2 Utilize Flowtivity to evaluate existing processes and leverage the collaborative Cloud based systems.		

Here's How to Get Your Road Map to Transform and Grow Your Accounting Firm...

You already know how to provide compliance services to your clients. The confusing part is not knowing how to migrate your CPA firm to providing the more lucrative advisory services clients crave.

That is where we come in. We help firms just like yours transform and grow their organization by providing a road map for leveraging advisory services in their firm.

Most people think it takes always adding new clients to their portfolio to grow their accounting firm.

Now you can transform and grow your accounting firm from the clients you already have.

If you would like us to help, just send an email to: Deanna.Perkins@Boomer.com and we will take it from there.

Visit www.Boomer.com/CAS to learn more about our advisory services consulting.

Visit www.Boomer.com/PC to learn about our community of firms and solution providers focused on leveraging technology and the cloud to provide higher-level client accounting services to their clients.

About the Author

L. Gary Boomer is CEO of Boomer Consulting, Inc., an organization that provides consulting services to leading accounting firms in the areas of Leadership & Management, Client Development, Talent Development, Technology and Compensation.

Gary is recognized in the accounting profession as the leading authority on technology and firm management. For over a decade, he has been named by Accounting Today as one of the 100 most influential people in accounting. He is also a member of IPA's 10 most recommended consultants.

He consults and speaks around the globe on management and technology related topics including strategic and technology planning, compensation, change management, and developing a training/learning culture. He acts as a planning facilitator, provides coaching, and serves on various advisory boards.

He is currently a member of the AICPA Life Insurance/ Disability Committee and the Accounting Advisory Board at Kansas State University. He recently served as president of the Kansas Society of CPAs and on the AICPA Council. He is also a member of The Advisory Board, a group that produces *Winning Is Everything*, the premier management conference. He is the past chairman of the AICPA's Information Technology Executive Committee and has also served on the AICPA's Academic and Career Development Executive Committee and the ACUTE Board of Directors.

Gary is the founder of The Boomer Technology Circles™, a community that helps firms bridge the gap between technology and practice management and accelerate their progress through thought leadership and peer accountability.

In addition to The Boomer Technology Circles™, Gary is the founder of the CIO Advantage, a community that prepares technology professionals for a seat at the management table by developing their business and IT acumen. Gary also created the CEO Advantage, a community of Managing Partners who act as a collaborative think tank to challenge, encourage, and propel each other to a higher level of success.

He is the author of *Performance³™* and a contributor to *The Boomer Advantage Guides* on:

☐   Strategic Planning

☐   Paperless Transition

☐   Human Capital Attraction & Retention

☐   Performance Management

☐   Mobile Security

☐   Training & Learning

☐ Implementing CRM

☐ Social Networking

☐ Business Continuation

☐ Succession Planning

☐ Partner Compensation

☐ Selection of a Managing Partner

☐ Client Filtering

☐ Risk Management in the Digital World

☐ Developing Managers

☐ Pricing for Value

☐ Electronic Confirmations

☐ Change Management

☐ Social Media

☐ Guide to Increased Profits and Cash Flow

Gary is the author of "Boomer's Blueprint," a monthly column in Accounting Today, and his team publishes the Boomer Bulletin™, a newsletter with worldwide circulation. He also contributes to *Think, Plan, Grow!* ™, Boomer Consulting's popular blog. In addition to consulting with hundreds of accounting firms, he has consulted with IBM, Microsoft, Intuit, CCH, and Thomson on the design and marketing of accounting related software and continues to consult with many industry technology providers to better serve the needs of the CPA profession.

Kolbe

L. Gary Boomer specializes in assessing rapidly changing circumstances while devising practical solutions. While he is willing to conduct some form of trial-and-error, he makes careful calculations to ensure the best possible outcomes. Gary is a highly capable communicator with a gift for taking complex matters and conveying them in a way that makes sense to a general audience. He is committed to maintaining pre-determined processes but is also a highly functioning improviser. He possesses a powerful, imaginative vision that carries him and his team to ever new and exciting possibilities.

Unique Abilities

L. Gary Boomer is a visionary leader who innately sees possibilities instead of road blocks. He is committed to the principles of teamwork and is willing to collaborate with individuals who may have very different working styles. Gary is highly intuitive and capable of getting to the heart of difficult issues while creating consensus. He gives deference to those around him and does not neglect to show loyalty to those who have earned it.

Personal

Mr. Boomer received his BS and MS degrees in accounting from Kansas State University. He and his wife Mary have three children, Jeff, Jim and Katie.